AT THE HORSE SHOW

With

MARGARET CABELL SELF

arco

New York

Acknowledgments

I should like to thank the officials of the Children's Services Show and of the Santa Barbara National Show for their kindness in helping to make this book possible. I should also like to thank those who contributed pictures and those who gave permission for their pictures to be used.

Published by ARCO PUBLISHING COMPANY, Inc.
219 Park Avenue South, New York, N.Y. 10003

Fourth Printing, 1977

Library of Congress Catalog Card Number 72-92310
ISBN 0-668-02747-9

Printed in the United States of America

Preface

The purpose of this book is to present, in photographs, as complete a picture as possible of the American horse show. These are candid shots, not posed, so that the reader may get an accurate idea of what goes on both in the ring and behind the scenes, and why. More than 600 photographs were taken by the author and those chosen were selected because each illustrates a special point of interest pertaining either to the horse, to the exhibitor, or to the general horse show scene.

The large majority of these pictures were taken at two of the country's largest and most representative shows, the Children's Services 15th Annual Horse Show given on the Polo Grounds at Farmington, Connecticut, and the Santa Barbara National Show at Santa Barbara, California. I chose these two shows for several reasons. First, because together they offered the largest variety of classes. Secondly, because one, the Farmington Show, is a country, all outdoor show laid in beautiful New England, while the Santa Barbara Show gives us the picture of a show which is held inside a city limits. As with many large horse shows, the Children's Services Show is organized by a group of hard working volunteers and given for charity, all proceeds over and above actual costs going to support their very fine organization. The Santa Barbara Show is the project of the Nineteenth District Agricultural Association of the State of California.

— MARGARET CABELL SELF

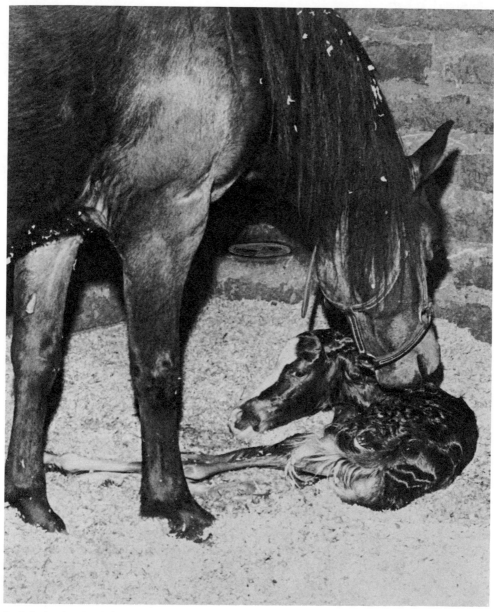

At birth the foal faces a strange world. What lies in store for him, whether he will make a name for himself in any one of the 22 divisions recognized by the American Horse Shows Association, remains to be seen. This will depend on his breeding, his training, and his own personal attributes. In any event, Saddler and Thorough- bred, Morgan, Quarter Horse and Shetland, Arabian and Appaloosa, all, like the five-minute-old foal shown here, will begin life with a thorough rubdown given by an attentive mother. This is the registered Welsh Mountain Pony mare Imperial Stately Acorn and her little filly Harvest Hill Easter Vigil.

Contents

1.

Giving a Show

PREPARATION OF GROUNDS

Preparations in Farmington, where the only permanent installations are the riding rings, start with the work of the ground crew. Here we see electricians setting up the communications lines which will later connect the stable areas, rings, judges' stands, announcer's booth, ambulance, fire-stations, police booth, and entrance gates.

Tents are rented to serve various purposes. Some are used as refreshment tents and others as tents for stabling. The latter are partitioned into roomy box stalls. A crew of men using motor equipment completes the erection of all tents the day before the show opens.

Setting up the outside course over which the hunters will compete is one of the biggest jobs of the ground crew. Jumps are constructed to exact specifications and the distance between each is measured to the inch.

The acres of grass, which are used for parking and schooling areas as well as the actual hunt course, are newly trimmed. Behind may be seen the completed stable tents, still empty of occupants. The rope and "wing" of natural wood in the foreground mark the edge of the outside hunt course.

Another major job is undertaken by a painting crew. All permanent fencing must be given a shiny new coat of white. Jumps and jump standards used for stadium jumping must also be refurbished.

On the day before the show is to open the first large (12-horse) van arrives and drives past the stable area to the unloading zone.

There the horses are unloaded, along with the tack (saddles, bridles, and other equipment). The now empty van is driven down and parked in the parking area reserved for the vans and trailers of the exhibitors.

The first job after the horse is un-loaded is to take off the tail bandages, which are worn to prevent the horse from rubbing the short hairs of his tail against the back of the stall in the van. Horses making long trips, especially when carried in less luxurious vans than this, often wear bandages on their legs as well.

Even before going to their assigned stalls the horses are mounted and taken out to the schooling areas to have a look at the hunt course so that they may become familiar with the layout. On the day of the show such schooling may not be feasible owing to the tight schedule of classes.

Not all the entries come in large vans. Here a local contestant takes her hunter out of a trailer which she has jeeped over. After schooling, he will be driven back to spend a peaceful night in his own stall.

Obstacles on the outside hunt course over which both horses and ponies will compete include (reading from left to right) gates painted gaily in red and white, poles and "aikens." Not shown are the "chicken coops," natural rails, hedges, and an in-and-out. Hunt course jumps differ from stadium-type obstacles in that they are supposed to represent the type of obstacle which might be met with in hunting. They are usually constructed in several heights which may or may not run next to each other. For horses there are two heights, 4' for "regular" (unclassified) horses and 3'6" for "green" (horses in their first two years of showing). A separate course for ponies is also set up. This may be completely separated from the obstacle for the horses or it may extend out from them. Again there are two different heights. Large ponies (over 13 hands) jump 3'. Those 13 hands and under jump 2'6". Junior hunters (those ridden by a junior) and small hunters (those not exceeding 15:2½ hands) take the "green" hunter course. This rider, schooling the day before the show, is Miss Jean Jennings on her mare Cover Girl. Tomorrow Miss Jennings will be formally dressed, wearing a hard hat, and Cover Girl will have her mane and tail in braids.

A rider shows a green pony an un-
familiar type of jump.

Then pops him over it.

Across the way from the outdoor course more exhibitors have arrived and are busy unpacking their equipment. The little two-wheeled vehicle on the pickup is called a "bike" and is used in certain harness classes. The four-wheeled vehicle is a "viceroy" and other types of ponies are driven hitched to this type of vehicle.

The opening day is bright with white clouds in a blue sky which add beauty to the lovely setting of the Farmington Children's Services Show. By now the parking area for exhibitors' cars, vans, and trailers is so crowded that there is little room left for late-comers.

SPECIAL EQUIPMENT AND SERVICES WHICH MUST BE PROVIDED AT ALL LARGE, RECOGNIZED SHOWS

There are many details pertaining to the comfort and safety of both the exhibitors and spectators which must be provided if the show is to be classed as an "Honor" show by the American Horse Shows Association. Water, both for the animals and for the exhibitors, is clearly an essential, and at the end of every section of stalls bottles of pure drinking water are provided while faucets are available for the filling of stable buckets. Public drinking troughs are no longer in favor as they are transmitters of that dread disease "shipping fever." Children of horse-minded parents soon learn their way around and roam the stables at will, generally without the need of supervision. They have been thoroughly trained in how to avoid trouble and how to stay out of danger.

A fire in the stable area is the most dreaded of all catastrophies. The stabling tents have been erected under strict fire prevention regulations so that in an emergency there will be available water and plenty of room for a fire engine to get close to the trouble spot. Meanwhile, the necessary fire fighting equipment remains parked nearby for the duration of the show. Public telephones are also provided, as well as temporary comfort stations.

Although serious accidents at horse shows are exceedingly rare, they do occasionally occur. This ambulance, which will remain on the grounds throughout the show, is now parked outside one of the rings where a jumping class is going on. When the hunters start over the outside course it will be moved to that area.

For minor casualties there is the First Aid trailer. Here we see the two nurses in charge trying to persuade a baby who has encountered a splinter to let them examine her finger.

The police, whose major job is that of directing traffic and seeing that parking and fire rules are obeyed, have their own trailer in the center of things. Here they chat with a rider from a neighboring stable who has ridden over with his dog to see what's going on.

Dust is one of the major problems, and several times during the morning and afternoon this water wagon appears and waters down the tracks in the rings as well as outside areas which have dried out.

HORSE SHOW EMPLOYEES AND OFFICIALS

Small shows usually have volunteers who place and remove the obstacles used in the stadium jumping classes. At larger shows such as this there is a paid crew to do this job. At the Children's Services Show, members of the governor's Horse Guards volunteer for the work; a contribution to the Guard is made by the show. Trailers hitched to tractors are used and the speed and dexterity of a trained crew do much to keep the show moving on schedule.

Every "A" rated show must have a blacksmith in constant attendance. Other shows should have one, and at a big show he will be kept busy. Generally he sets his forge up under a special tent and horses requiring attenton are brought to him there. But where time is essential he may tighten a loose shoe just before a horse enters a class, or, in an emergency, even enter the ring and do his repairs there. The latter would occur only in the case of horses being shown on the flat. Jumpers and hunters, if they have the misfortune to lose a shoe while in competition, may either continue without it or withdraw from the class. Shoeing is all-important and varies greatly with the type of horse or pony being exhibited. Those which must show high action such as the saddlers and harness ponies wear heavy shoes and thick pads. There is a limit as to how heavy these may be, however, and according to the AHSA

rules an exhibitor may protest the footgear of a competitor. In such a case, the exhibitor against whom the protest is made may either withdraw his entry or, in the presence of a veterinarian, may have the shoes and pads removed and weighed to settle the dispute.

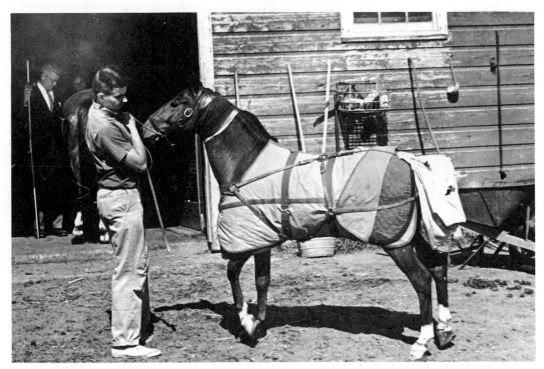

Ponies are classified according to their height. This applies to all types of ponies — harness, hunter and "pet." When first entering competition they must be measured by an official veterinarian. Ponies under six years are measured each year and a temporary card, good for the duration of the year, is issued. After the age of six a permanent card is issued. In measuring, the veterinarian sees that the animal's head is sufficiently lowered so that the highest point of the withers is obvious, and it is at this point that the animal is measured. He must be standing on a level floor and the measurement is given in "hands." There are four inches to a hand. At the time of measuring, the veterinarian makes a note of the type of shoe the pony is wearing, his height, and the height of the foot of the animal at the heel as well as the length of his toe. High-actioned animals wearing thick pads and heavy shoes often have long toes, but there is a limit as to how long the toe of a pony or a horse is permitted to be for exhibition purposes. Here we see the veterinarian measuring a hunter pony while a harness pony in "wraps" waits outside. In addition to his job of measuring, the veterinarian may be called upon to decide questions of soundness of eye, wind, or limb of a given animal. It should be noted that once entered, an animal is not permitted to withdraw from a class and ask a return of his entry fee on the grounds of unsoundness without the supporting word of the veterinarian.

It is the duty of the Ring Steward to measure the height of each jump after the course has been set up. If during the competition a bar is misplaced, the Ring Steward must make certain that it is correctly replaced. Other duties include repeating the orders given to the competitors in the class by the judge, relaying the list of winners to the announcer at the public address system, and making himself generally useful.

Clarence "Honey" Craven is the all-important Horse Show Manager. His work starts many days before the opening of the show, for it is he who decides on such details as the sequence of the classes, and settles all the problems which arise regarding the exhibitors, their needs and wishes. It is he who puts the show on the road and keeps it running smoothly. For many years "Honey" served as Ring Master and tooted the long horn, where his kind face and helpful ways became familiar to all. Behind him stands the class caller, Steve Lusco. With two rings and the outside course to keep going, the class caller is an important assistant to the regular announcer.

In traditional coaching costume—gray topper, scarlet coat trimmed with yellow and leather puttees—the Ringmaster, G. Webster Brown, puts his long golden horn to his lips and announces the opening of the show.

No person may judge at a Recognized Horse Show unless he has been issued a Judge's Card by the AHSA which states that he is qualified to judge that particular division. The two gentlemen we see here are Daniel H. Conway from Oswego, N.Y., and Earl "Red" Frazier from Atlanta, Georgia. They are outside the judge's stand on the outside course at the Farmington Show, concentrating on the performance of a Hunter Class and obviously pleased with what they see. Included each year in the AHSA rule book is a complete list of registered judges with their addresses.

Mrs. Robert Rost of Branchville, New Jersey, was one of three Recognized Judges chosen to decide the winners in the jumper classes. Although conformation, manners, way of going, etc. are not considered in jumper classes, touches, knockdowns, refusals, and so forth must be penalized according to specified regulations and it is up to the judge to decide when such a penalty has been merited and to write the score of each contestant down on his judges' card.

Spectators at shows come in many sizes, ages, and costumes. The area around the rings at most outdoor shows is divided into parking spaces, with folding chairs along the fence. In this way quite a bit of additional money can be raised and those willing to pay for the privilege are assured a choice location from which to view the show. Each ring also has bleachers open to the public.

SPECTATORS

Not all spectators are human. These two Harlequins seem to take a real interest in what goes on.

One of the youngest spectators was Sara, aged four months, who is shown riding papoose fashion on the back of her mother, Mrs. James Shea.

Young visitors who are not yet good enough horsemen to enter as exhibitors and too old to be carried "piggy-back" have a special horse section all their own at Farmington. This is the "pony-ride ring," where for a small fee an exciting dash around an enclosed arena on a specially trained mount may be enjoyed.

Since ponies are notorious "nippers," and since the clientele may not be educated in such matters, all ponies wear muzzles. They are so well trained that the starter has only to set them on the course with a mild whack on the buttocks and they travel once around, coming to a stop at the end with no further supervision. This young lady, whose feet don't quite make the stirrups, is asking if her pony will only trot or if there's a chance of a canter.

We go now to the Santa Barbara National Show. The show grounds occupy a number of acres and the buildings are permanent, in contrast to those in Farmington. The main building is a large, open-air arena surrounded by a covered visitors gallery. Outside stands a wagon with a patient wooden horse showing a display of china by the Metlox Company.

Along the drive are placed other vehicles of earlier times. These will be driven into the ring at intervals during the show to entertain the spectators and add variety to the show.

36

Behind the enclosed arena is a large schooling area and beyond that an outdoor ring with a covered spectators' gallery. In the distance can be seen one of the van and trailer parking areas.

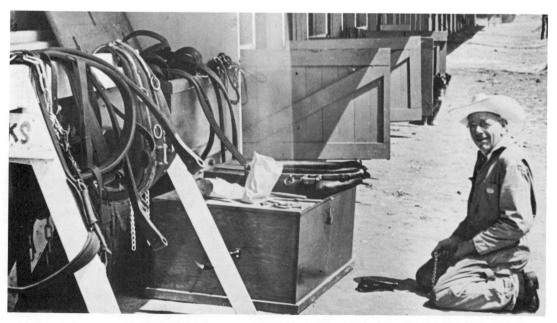

E. J. Paul of the Metlox (Poppytrail) Pottery Company of Manhattan Beach, California, makes minor repairs to the harness of the teams which are driven in the various exhibitions put on by this company at the Santa Barbara Show.

Further along we come to the fire engine that will later make its daring run to the delight of the audience. Of shining, polished brass and "fireman red" enamel, it is one of the last such vehicles to remain in working condition. It weighs three tons and pumps 750 gallons of water a minute. In a later section of this book will be found a complete sequence of pictures showing the fire engine in operation.

Another vehicle owned by the Metlox Company and used by them in their exhibition is this four-horse hitch of Hackney horses which is being readied outside one of the arenas.

The color gray in hunters is a favorite for it catches the judge's eye and is particularly becoming to the rider wearing a "pink" coat. Unfortunately gray horses show stable stain more than do those of other colors, and daily baths are often a necessity. This hunter seems resigned to the ordeal and stands quietly in his coat of suds while the groom works away on a fetlock.

Stall space is allotted according to the breed of horse. Thus exhibitors of like interest are grouped together and, when it is necessary for interested friends to find them their location is made easy. These horses of the Blakiston Ranch will be shown in the Hunter and Thoroughbred divisions. Riders shown here wearing hunting livery are waiting to go into an Appointments class. Notice the matching tack trunks painted in the colors and with the initials of the stable; also the row of ribbons which go on display as soon as the tack area is set up.

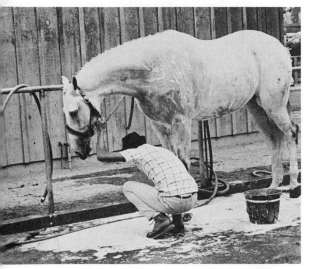

Many stables bring complete tents in bright colors in which equipment can be kept away from dust. The Peacock Hill Riding Club evidently likes the American Saddle Horses rather than the hunters and displays pictures of its winners. Behind, a groom works on a saddle, for tack must be soaped and polished each time it is used.

The Tennessee Walking Horse is another member of the American Saddle clan. This horse is coming in from the exercising arena. His tail is still in his stable bandage. Notice the band of metal on the outside of the hoof to strengthen the wall, and the rubber "bell" boots to protect the coronet from injury. The bit has a curved shank and is the type used on most walking horses.

Tied to the back of the bleachers at the end of the outdoor arena stands a row of ponies waiting for the veterinary to measure them.

Saddle and harness horses are taught very early in life to "camp" or "stretch." Originally this was for the protection of ladies unable to move quickly because of their voluminous skirts. The carriage horse was put in this "stretching" position while the ladies entered or left the vehicle; he could not move forward or backward without first getting his feet under him. This is a young Shetland waiting to enter an "In Hand" class.

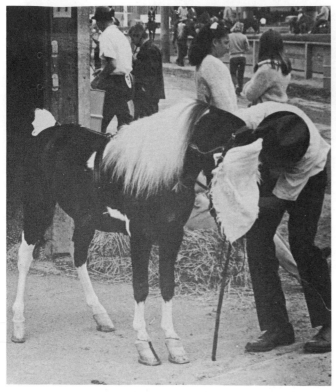

Around the corner waits a miniature Shetland stallion, Mr. Kewpie Doll. He wears a veil to counteract his roving eye. This picture shows clearly the length of toe which these ponies wear. I was told that on some the shoe and pad of each foot weighed more than 40 ounces.

The aisles between the rows of stalls give plenty of room for exercising. This is a Hackney pony being warmed up for a class.

A Saddle Horse is being led to the blacksmith tent to have his shoes checked. The tack tent is adorned with the long tails of championship ribbons, and the little "bikes" of the harness ponies are upended against the stall.

The enclosed arena is ample in size. In the center is a judges' stand on wheels kept decorated with flowers from the flower show which in another building runs in conjunction with the horse show. To save time, a class of conformation hunters is being judged on one side of the ring while a class of Stock horses, which have already performed, wait for the judge's final decision on the other.

2.
Breeding, Model and Conformation Classes

These classes are often referred to as "in hand" classes because the animal is not shown with a rider or hitched to an appropriate vehicle but is led into the ring by an exhibitor on foot.

Each division (hunter, Morgan, Arabian, Palomino, etc.) has special requirements for horses or ponies showing in "in hand" classes and these will be examined in more detail as each such division is discussed. Generally speaking, horses competing in breeding classes must be registered in the registration book of that breed. Model classes do not necessarily require such registration, nor do the "conformation" classes. The latter type of class is usually a part of a performance class; thus in "conformation hunters" the horse is first shown over the hunt course and is then stripped and brought in to be judged on his conformation (general build and physical attributes) and soundness.

Breeding classes are often divided as to sex and age, and there will be classes for stallions, for geldings, and for mares, as well as for foals, yearlings, two-, three- and four-year-old colts. Model classes may be divided as to sex, age, or height. The division of conformation classes follows the rules pertaining to hunters. In Green Conformation Hunters classes conformation counts 50 to 40 per cent of the total score, whereas in Regular Conformation it counts 40 to 30 per cent. There may also be Ladies Conformation Hunters, Appointment, and Conformation Hunter Hack classes; in these categories conformation counts 25 per cent.

THOROUGHBRED AND CONFORMATION HUNTER

A yearling filly, Flora McFlimsey, by Charlevoix out of Mad Madge by Hilltown, stands waiting to be judged in a breeding class limited to yearlings. She is owned and was bred by the Tanrackin Farm of Bedford Hills, New York.

The judge walks down the line in a model class for Thoroughbred mares.

Conformation hunters in an appointments class having jumped have now been stripped and will be judged on conformation and soundness.

Jogging for soundness.

Sutton Place ridden by Champ Hough and owned by Mr. and Mrs. Zellerback of Menlo Park, California, was later moved to the head of the line and pinned first.

THE ARABIAN

The Arabian is the progenitor of all modern light horse breeds. To some it may seem hard to believe that horses of such divergent types as the Thoroughbred, American Saddle, and Quarter Horse go back to a common ancestral breed, but so it is and we may thank the importers of the three Arabian stallions, the Godolphin Barb, the Darley Arabian, and the Byerley Turk, for the quality of the horses competing in the shows today. Though the Thoroughbred can outrun the Arabian, due to his longer legs inherited from the English mares from which he is descended, it is to the Arabian blood in his veins that he owes his spirit, his alertness, and his running ability. The horses imported by the Spanish invaders were of Arabian blood, and it is from them that the Western mustangs developed, and the stock horse of today owes his strength, dexterity, and strong bone structure to these same Spanish ancestors. Furthermore, horse breeders soon learned that the introduction of Arabian blood tended to improve the quality of all types of horses and ponies, so we find Hackneys, Welsh ponies, and many other breeds developing refinement and intelligence through the introduction of such blood. There will always be those who contend that of all breeds the "pure breds," as the Arabian Horse Association prefers to designate its breed, make the most delightful riding horses and are the most intelligent, cooperative, and gentle of all, and I for one would certainly never deny it. Also, this is one of the most versatile of breeds being shown in successful competition as trail, stock, and pleasure horse under Western tack, as jumper, bridlepath hack, and general pleasure horse under English tack. They have also made a name for themselves in such competitions as the Vermont Trail Ride and other endurance tests. Of all the modern breeds, the Arabian looks the most like his ancestors of 200 hundred years ago and, though there are breeders who would like to see him ape some of the other types, let us hope that he is kept as his desert masters wanted him, a powerful, finely boned animal with a magnificent crest and throttle; a delicate, concave head; full, widely set eye; sloping shoulder; short back (the Arabian has one fewer vertebra than other breeds); a fairly level croup; a natural mane and tail, the former neither hogged, braided, nor shortened, the latter neither tortured and disfigured by operations nor added to; and a beautiful floating gait not interfered with by excessive weight in his shoes or additional length to his toes.

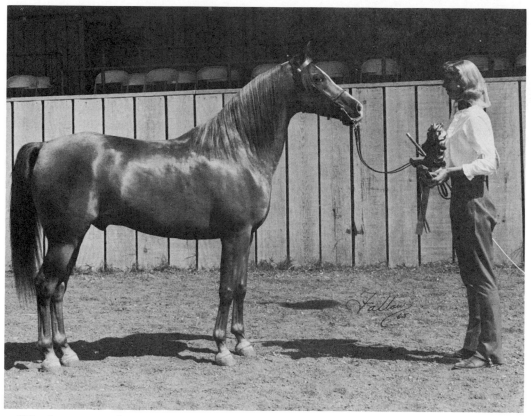

We do not need a program to tell us that this is a fine example of an Arabian being shown in a breeding class. Note the beautifully cut out throttle and the short back. (Photo by June Fallaw)

One of the distinguishing features of the five-gaited Saddler is his long, flowing mane. As shown here, the foretop and the first ten inches or so of mane are braided into pigtails which hang straight. The ribbon used is often colored and the bridle usually has a colored browband to match. This chestnut gelding waiting to be judged is Wild Wind, registered number 20175. He is 15:3 hands, six years old, and is owned by the Glenburn Valley Farm of Princeton, New Jersey.

THE AMERICAN SADDLE HORSE DIVISION

The Saddler was developed in colonial times from English Thoroughbred stock by the plantation owners in Kentucky, Virginia, and other southern states. The goal was an animal with the flash and fire of the Thoroughbred but with a more comfortable gait. The foundation sire was the famous stallion Denmark. There are two types of American Saddle Horses—those which are required to show three gaits (the walk, trot, and canter) and those which must show five (the above gaits plus a "slow gait" and a "rack"). More detailed descriptions of these gaits will be found in the "Performance Class" section of this book. In the model and breeding classes the horses are shown in hand in either a halter or a bridle and are judged on conformation, finish, soundness, and natural action at the trot. No more than two attendants per animal are permitted in the ring.

Royal Command, a chestnut stallion, 16 hands, four years old, registered number 42542, is owned by Cedar Ledge Farm of Wethersfield, Connecticut. He is posing in the "stretching" or "camping" position peculiar to Saddlers, harness horses, and ponies.

Another distinguishing feature of the five-gaited Saddler is his sweeping tail. but it is astounding how nature can be encouraged to develop a trait such as this. This beautiful bay gelding, King of the Road, is receiving a well-deserved blue. He is 15:3, aged eight years, and is owned by Mr. and Mrs. John Tracy of West Simsbury, Connecticut.

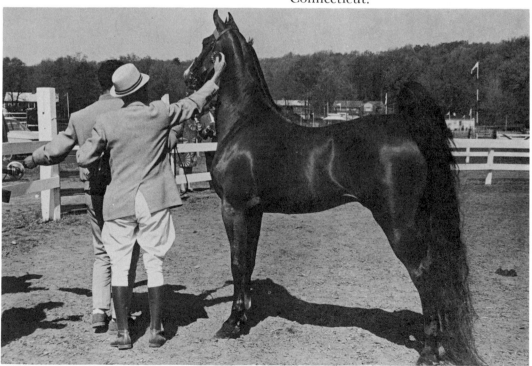

The three-gaited Saddler has a more scanty tail than his five-gaited brother. It is usually thinned at the dock and then brushed out below. Although there has been a great deal of discussion and efforts on the part of humane societies to prevent the artificial "setting" of the Saddler's tail, this practice is still almost universal. Here we see Dainty Majestic, a five-year-old chestnut mare, 15:1½ hands owned by the Frosty Hollow Farm of Hamden, Connecticut. She has just won her model class and is posing for the photographers outside the ring at Farmington.

TENNEESEE WALKING HORSE DIVISION

The "Walking Horse" is a cousin of the American Saddler, both having been developed from the same strains. At first he was purely a utility horse, his principal work being to carry his master through the fields and between the rows of crops without stepping on the latter. Speed was not essential nor was the extreme sensitivity of the Thoroughbred and the Kentucky Saddle Horse desirable, but smoothness of gait was highly valued, as the plantation owner often spent four or five hours at a stretch in the saddle. These horses are required to show only the flat-footed walk, the "running walk," and the slow canter. It is the second of these gaits, the "running walk," which is their distinguishing characteristic and from which they take the name of "Plantation Walkers." The Tennessee Walking Horse Association is one of the more recently organized, having been established in 1935.

A fine example of the Walking Horse was this seven-year-old black mare, My Little Margie, owned by Mrs. Ben McBurney. In comparing these horses to the American Saddle Horse it will be noticed that they have somewhat heavier necks and are deeper through the heart.

53

The winner of the class was Becky
Allen of the Merrywood Farm, Red-
lands, California. Another picture of
Becky Allen is shown in Chapter One.

QUARTER HORSE DIVISION

The American Quarter Horse was developed in colonial times by the plantation owners in Virginia. At that time there were no race tracks. The country was wooded and the country roads rarely ran straight for more than a quarter of a mile. It became the custom for riders to challenge their friends to short races over this distance where the footing permitted. Thus a horse that was a quick starter but one that did not need to be much of a stayer was developed. He was called a "Quarter Horse" because of the distance which he was called upon to run, not, as many people believe, because his outstanding feature is the tremendous muscular development of his hindquarters. The foundation sire of the breed was an imported Thoroughbred stallion named Janus.

The muscles of a Quarter Horse differ from those of the Thoroughbred and Saddle strains, being bulkier and thus bulging. This is especially noticeable in the jaw. The American Horse Show Association defines good conformation in the Quarter Horse as calling for a relatively short head, wide at the jaw and between the eyes, but with a small muzzle and a shallow, firm mouth. Nostrils must be full and sensitive, ears short and alert, eyes large, jaws well developed with much width between the bottom edges, neck not unduly short with a trim throttle or throat latch (not hammer headed) and not too heavy where it joins the head. The neck should blend into sloping shoulders with good withers which should be the same height as the croup. The chest must be deep and broad with legs set well apart, the forearms well muscled, gaskins and thighs close coupled, strong back and loin, well sprung ribs, short, broad, flat cannons with firm ankles and good pasterns, not too straight or long and sloping. The feet should be tough with a wide heel and well-developed frog. In other words, this horse, which today is most valuable as a working member of a stock ranch, must show by his conformation that he can carry weight and has the stamina, quickness, and strength to earn his keep. He may run from 14:3 hands to 15:1 (though some may run a little over or under this height), and most weigh from 1,100 to 1,300 pounds. Any color is permitted except spotted horses.

55

A Quarter Horse breeding class lines
up. On the other side of the arena a
class of Thoroughbred mares is being
judged.

This sorrel Quarter Horse shows the
well-developed quarters as well as the
prominently bulging arm muscles.

This palomino Quarter Horse has a
good head and good muscular development, especially around the upper arm
and gaskin. His back is perhaps a little
long.

This bay stallion has a well cut out
throttle. The depth of jaw from the
eye down is not as deep as in some,
nor are the haunches as well developed.

PALOMINO DIVISION

The eligibility for registry of the Palomino horse is determined not by blood lines but by color. Membership in either of two breeders' associations makes the horse eligible for showing — the Palomino Horse Breeders Association of America, and the Palomino Horse Association of Chatsworth, California. To be eligible the animal must have, as nearly as possible, a body color which is within three shades of the color of a newly minted coin. The mane and tail must be full, fine, and pure white, and the color must be natural, not bleached. The horse may have white socks or stockings or white markings on the face, but any white on the body above the knees or hocks is penalized in the show ring. The eyes may be either hazel or dark brown, but must both be of the same color. They may not have light blue, pink, or "glass" eyes. In breeding classes the color counts 50 per cent, general conformation finish, soundness, and ability to move correctly on the line the remaining 50. Since Palominos may be of any breed, ·the conformation of the individual horses will vary. Arabian, American Saddle, and Quarter Horses often are shown in the same class. The judge must decide which is the best animal of its type. In shows where many entries are expected, the classes may specify the type of Palomino. Unlike most classes for horses, Palominos may be as small as 14 hands and should not be larger than 16. Heavily weighted shoes and long toes are discouraged.

A class of mixed type Palominos assembles as the judge enters the ring. Reading from right to left we see what might be an Arabian, then a Palomino Saddle Horse, while the two on the left probably have a good deal of Quarter Horse ancestry.

Goldmounts Beauty the Quarter Horse type on the left, took the class. She is a four-year-old mare owned by Dominic Bressi of San Luis Obispo, California. The other mare in the picture, Timona, owned by Al Garcia, of El Cajon, California placed second. This was a class for Palomino mares, any type.

Belvelier's Golden Belle poses for the judge. She is a ten-year-old mare, owned by Edna Fagen of Chatsworth, California. She comes from the famous Peavine (American Saddle Horse) family.

In the class for geldings, Playboy's Golden Dream also owned by Dominic Bressi, showed how long a tail could be grown if one really tried.

PINTO DIVISION

The Pinto division is the most recently recognized by the AHSA. Like the Appaloosa and the Palomino this is a color breed. Registration in the Association is determined by the color of the coat. The Pinto Horse Association classifies its horses as Overos or Tobianos. The former are described as horses that are, primarily, some color other than white, with dark mane and tail, and with irregular white splashy markings. The Tobiano shows a clearly marked pattern with white as a base and another color, preferably divided half and half throughout the coat; the mane and tail should be the color of the part of the body from which they stem. Horses may be of any breed and their conformation should display the qualities desirable in that breed. They may be shown in performance classes of all kinds when they conform to the rules regarding tack, appointments, and performance as required for that particular class. The name "Pinto," which means "painted" in Spanish, was adopted for the name of this breed because it covered horses of both piebald (black and white) and skewbald (white with any color other than black) markings. In Ireland such horses are called "colored" horses, as are Appaloosas. In the West they have also been known as "spotted" horses and "calico" horses or "paints."

A Pinto breeding class for mares. The first three mares and the last in line show the Tobiano coloring, the fourth and fifth the Overa. (Photo by Ray M. Watson)

61

PONY DIVISION

To many spectators the Pony Division is the most appealing. Breeders, having found that there is a very good market for ponies of all types and breeds, have set high standards and are spending thousands of dollars in blooded stock to uphold and improve these standards. Prices of prize-winning and of untried ponies with promising futures have soared and pony classes in all categories are well filled. Generally speaking a pony is an animal of the equine race not over 14:2 hands in height (58" measured at the withers), but there are many exceptions to this rule. Quarter Horses, Arabians, Stock Horses, and Morgans may all be under 14:2 (though not under 14.) In all divisions ponies are classified as "small," not exceeding 13 hands, and "large," over 13 but not exceeding 14:2 (Welsh not to exceed 14 hands). In the case of pony hunters and jumpers they may be divided into three divisions: not exceeding 11:2 to jump 2'; over 11:2 and not exceeding 13 to jump 2'6", and over 13 to jump 3'. The measurement for Shetland ponies differs from the above in that in this division the small division is open to ponies 10:3 (43") in height and the large to those over 10:3 and not exceeding 11:2 (46"). All ponies in all divisions must have official cards from the AHSA giving their exact heights before they will be allowed to enter the ring.

PONY HUNTERS

As in the Hunter Division, conformation pony hunters are not required to be of any one specific breed and are judged on their conformation with regard to their suitability as a child's hunter. These ponies are generally of mixed breeding, having Welsh, Thoroughbred, Arabian, Irish and other types of pony blood in different combinations. Many are imported from Ireland and England each year and those being bred here are usually of imported stock. The aim of the breeders is to produce a miniature horse rather than an animal with marked pony characteristics, hence the generous infusion of Thoroughbred and Arabian bloodlines. Fineness is desirable, but, since they are to carry a child over fences in the hunt field, substance is equally important. To increase interest in the breeding and training of pony hunters there is an annual competition called the International Pony Competition. Those children whose ponies make the team are eligible to represent the United Sttaes in team competition against foreign countries. The team is chosen from the small and large pony divisions, the winners being the ponies that have racked up the most points in the International Pony Classes.

Conformation pony hunters, having jumped the outside course, are judged on conformation and soundness at the Children's Services Show. Note the beautiful braiding job on the gray in the foreground.

Formality and politeness are a part of the horse-show picture. The judge tips his hat to the young exhibitor of Midget, owned by the Greenbriar Farm of Lakeville, Connecticut, as he asks her to move her entry farther forward in the line.

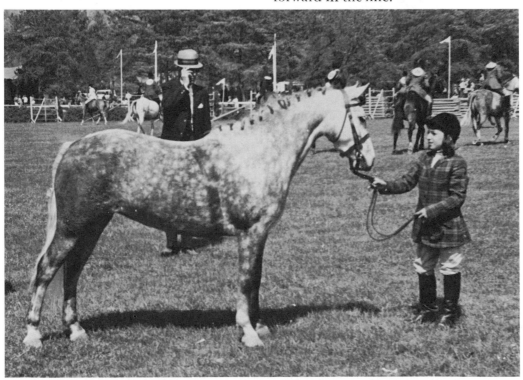

A somewhat different type of pony is this sturdy specimen which, by his build and calmness, could probably carry his young rider comfortably and safely in any type of country. He is Campbell Kid, owned and shown by Robert Stearnes.

HACKNEY PONY

The Hackney Pony is the miniature counterpart of the Hackney Horse, that valued road horse whose ancestry can be traced back to the year 1495. So highly thought of were these animals that an act of the English Legislature forbade their deportation except with the express permission of the king. The Hackney Horse made his name as a puller of fast coaches, as a gentleman's Saddler, and as the horse that his owner either "hacked" to the hunt or drove between the shafts of his dog-cart with his hunter hitched tandem in the lead. When horses were put off the road by the advent of the motor vehicles, the Hackney, which in the United States had been largely replaced as a saddle mount by the American Saddle Horse, still retained his place in sporting coaches and dog carts, but became rare. However, the Hackney Pony retained his popularity in the show ring. Until recently all registered Hackneys were shown as such, wearing docked tails. Ponies with long tails, very often pure Hackney, were shown as "Harness Ponies."

Of recent years, since the classes have become more and more popular, large Hackneys may be shown in breeding classes with long tails and then go on to show in harness classes as well. The latest edition of the AHSA Rule Book takes care not to state in its breeding section for Hackneys that, as in former years, breeding stock must have the short tail. Classes may be divided as to heights, all entries must be registered in the American Hackney Horse Society, and in the breeding and model classes they are judged on conformation, type, quality, and finish.

Glen Orbit, bay Hackney Stallion, age three, is shown by Julie Hawley of Santa Barbara in a class for Hackney Pony stallions three years old or over.

65

WELSH MOUNTAIN PONY

Of all breeds of ponies, the Welsh has earned the reputation of being the prettiest, best tempered, most versatile, and most suitable for the child to show, ride, hunt, jump, or drive. The Welsh Pony and Cob Society, with the aid of the AHSA, is doing its best to see that their breed remains a true child's pony with natural head and tail carriage and natural gaits, and that he stands naturally and quietly. For this reason tail irritants and braces are forbidden, length of toe is limited, shoes and pads together may not weigh more than ten ounces, ponies must stand squarely on all four feet with the toes of the hind feet no farther back than the quarter, and only one attendant may exhibit a pony. Welsh ponies must be no higher than 14 hands and all classes must be divided into "A" and "B" sections. "A" section ponies may not exceed 12:2 hands; "B" section ponies are over 12:2 but must not exceed 14 hands. Any color is acceptable except piebald (black and white) or skewbald (any color other than black with white). Since the Welsh are known to have a good deal of Arabian blood, a slight "dish" in the profile of the head is desirable, as are bold, wide-set eyes and small, pointed ears, resulting in an overall delicate appearance of the head. The specifications as to desirable conformation emphasize substance, requiring a deep girth, well-sprung limbs, and a muscular back and loins, but the quarters must be lengthy and not "cobby" or blocky. In mares and geldings the neck should be lengthy, well carried and moderately lean, but in stallions it should be inclined to be cresty. Many classifications of breeding classes are listed with the division between "junior" ponies and "senior" ponies, three years being the age at which stallions are required to be fully developed.

Harvest Hill Charter Oak, owned and shown by Mrs. David Wells, has won many ribbons and stands a good chance of being placed first in this class also.

A line of Welsh pony stallions, three years old and over, being judged at Santa Barbara.

Davric Rock and Roll, also owned by
Mrs. Wells, presents the picture that
comes most quickly to mind on hear-
ing the term "Welsh Pony," for of all
colors gray is by far the most popular.

SHETLAND PONY

Of all the modern breeds of horses and ponies, the Shetlands have changed the most in appearance and in purpose. Originally from the Shetland Isles, these ponies were built like little cart horses with tremendously powerful shoulders, short, heavy necks, and square hindquarters. They were first used to pull the coal carts in the coal mines. Later they were bred and trained to pull "governess" carts and to carry the youngest children to the hunt wearing seats made of basketware.

In America the English-type Shetlands were considered too slow and stocky to make good children's mounts and they had a bad reputation for stubbornness. An American-type Shetland then emerged, having strains of Hackney and sometimes Arabian blood which had been introduced to fine down the stocky little pony and give him longer legs. Because these ponies were still intended to be ridden and driven by children, their feet were kept trimmed and no attempt was made to give them specially high action.

About 30 years ago breeders became interested in developing the Shetland as a high-stepping harness pony. More Hackney blood was introduced, toes were grown out, weighted shoes and heavy pads became the thing to wear, and the pony was trained to stretch and to move like a Hackney. It is this type of Shetland that is being shown today and though without a doubt he is a smarter looking pony than the little fellow that drew the coal carts or his American cousin, many people regret that his high spirit generally makes the modern version unsuitable as a pet or a child's companion. This is not always true, however, and many breeding farms train and encourage the stock not destined for the show ring for children's mounts. Of course, many of the tiny ones are too small to be really useful, but they are certainly enchanting little fellows with their manes and tails like silk and their tiny ears and slender muzzles. Also the breeding stock brings enormous prices!

Shetland classes may be divided as to size (under 43 in. and 43 to 46 in.), as to age, or as to sex. This class is one for yearling and two-year-old stallions. Though color does not count, breeders are particularly interested in unusual color combinations such as the pony in the foreground, which is a "chocolate" with flax mane and tail.

Pony stallions may be shown in "tack" consisting of leather surcingle with crupper strap and check reins as shown here. Pony mares may not be shown in anything other than a bridle or halter. If a stallion is shown in tack, checks must be removed before the final decision is made.

Another unusual two-toned color combination is this pale gray pony with a dark mane and tail. He is being shown "stripped," without tack, yearling stallions, like mares, not being permitted to wear anything other than a bridle or halter.

This is a somewhat older stallion being shown at the trot. His name is Daley's Golden Comet, a chestnut, 45 inches high, belonging to Dr. Gladys Wackerli. Notice the high action both in front and behind.

Trotting back, Daley's Golden Comet
again shows good form.

Mr. Kewpie Doll, the little stallion
shown wearing the veil in Chapter 1,
stands nicely and has the well-
developed muscles and fine head that
the judges like.

But when shown on the line he was inclined to play . . .

. . . and on returning to his place seemed to be arguing with his trainer. Nevertheless, in the championship class he was pinned reserve.

The championship went to this beautiful little brown stallion, Fernwood Frisco Model II, registered number 76186, owned by Mr. and Mrs. Robert Balding. He has the high withers, sloping shoulders, well-sprung ribs and well-rounded barrel, the short back and strong loin with a nearly level croup, and the refined, expressive head that are the desired characteristics of the modern-day Shetland.

3.
Performance Classes

A performance class is one in which the horse (or pony) is required to "perform" and show what he can do according to his breed and training. Jumpers and hunters are shown over obstacles; saddle horses, stock horses, hacks, etc., are shown on the flat under saddle. Fine harness, roadsters, and some others such as Morgans are shown to appropriate vehicles. In every case specific rules have been laid out as to what is the ideal performance, what constitutes a bad performance and must be penalized by the judges, and what types of courses, gaits, and so on are required for horses or ponies showing in that particular division. These points and others will be covered in detail as each division in the performance class is pictured.

Hunter Division

Performance Hunters. Performance Hunters are classified as "Green" and "Regular." A Green Hunter is one that is in his first or second calendar year of competition over jumps 3' or higher. A Regular Hunter is one that has finished his Green years of competition and is in his third or later year of competition. Hunters are further classified as "Conformation Hunters," "Working Hunters," "Qualified Hunters," and "Junior Hunters." All hunters are judged on soundness and performance. The latter includes manners, jumping style, way of moving, and the maintenance of an even hunting pace. In Conformation Hunters the quality and substance of the animal is also judged.

Hunters need not be Thoroughbred though there are often classes limited to Thoroughbred Hunters, and most modern hunters are at least half Thoroughbred. Qualified Hunters are those which have hunted at least one season with a registered pack; when registering for such a class, the owner must present a card from the Master of Foxhounds of that pack so stipulating. Junior Hunters are hunters ridden by a junior who has not reached the age of eighteen. In the following classes, as well as the two last mentioned, entries may be judged either as Conformation or as Working Hunters, this being stated in the Prize List. Such additional classes include "Ladies to Ride" and "Amateurs to Ride" classes in which manners are to be emphasized; in "Corinithian" and "Appointments" classes, where riders must wear hunt livery and the horse special tack and equipment, brilliance is emphasized. Horses may also be classified according to size- or weight-carrying ability such as "Small Hunters" (not to exceed 15:2½ hands,) "Lightweight" (carrying up to 165 lbs.); "Middleweight" (carrying up to 185 lbs.); and "Heavyweight" (carrying up to 205 lbs.). There are also classes which divide the hunters according to experience and previous winnings. These include "Maiden," "Novice," and "Limit Hunters," i.e., those who have not won a blue ribbon, three blue ribbons, or six blue ribbons respectively. One further classification is that of "Young Hunters," open to horses five years old and under.

Obstacles on the hunt course vary according to the classification of the horse. Green Hunters in their first year of showing, Junior Hunters, Young Hunters and Maiden, Novice, and Limit Hunters jump a maximum height of 3'6". In his second year of showing, the Green Hunter is asked to jump 3'9". Regular Hunters jump 4' minimum in Class "A," and "B" sections, 3'9". In "C" sections for local and camp shows there is no minimum. The above section-letters relate to a point scoring system set up by the AHSA whereby a record is kept of the winnings of every Regular Hunter throughout the season. At the end of the year the horse with the most points is declared Horse of the Year. The same records are kept for horses in other divisions as well.

In addition to being judged on manners, way of going, etc., a horse is penalized if it has a "fault" when jumping. Fault penalties are as follows:

Knockdowns

An obstacle whose height is lowered is considered a knockdown.

1. A knockdown by any part of the horse's body behind the stifle	2 faults
2. A knockdown by any part of the body in front of the stifle	4 faults
3. A knockdown of standard or wing by any part of horse's body or rider	4 faults
4. Placing a foot in a Liverpool or water jump	4 faults

Disobediences

These include run-outs, refusals, bolting on course, extra circles.

1st disobedience	**3 faults**
2nd disobedience	**6 faults**
3rd disobedience	Elimination

Jumping an obstacle before it is reset, bolting from the ring, failure to keep a proper course, jumping an obstacle not on course, and fall of horse or rider also mean elimination. It should be noted that in the event of a refusal which occurs in an in-and-out type of obstacle (an obstacle consisting of more than one element which must be taken separately,) after the refusal or run-out the horse must not retake both elements of the jump, as is necessary in jumping classes, but must start over the element at which the disobedience occurred.

The shows which give the hunter of any classification the best opportunity to show his worth are those which have an outside course. Here we see the beautiful gray Thoroughbred hunter Polish Fiddler, owned by the Cavcote Farm of Glen Head, Long Island. He is shown taking the Aiken, a favorite type of obstacle, composed of rails and brush.

One of the advantages that the outside hunt course has over the inside course is that the judges have a chance to see the horse move out between jumps and then be steadied by the rider as he approaches his next fence.

Little Fiddle, owned by the My Play Stable of Guilderland, New York, is shown taking the brush jump in a Junior Hunter class at Farmington.

The fences used in a course for hunters set up in a ring such as shown here in the Santa Barbara Arena are supposed to resemble as closely as possible obstacles which a hunter is apt to encounter in the field. These include chicken coops (with or without extra bars on top which are known as "riders"), gates, post-and rail-fences, imitation stone and brick walls, etc., but would not include painted barrels, striped poles, triple bars, or other obstacles which are typical of courses set up for jumpers.

Artemis, a brown mare owned by the Provincial Realty Company of Rolling Hills, California, and ridden by Lark Ellison, shows good hunter form over a gate set in a simulated stone wall.

79

The favorite type of bridle for a hunter is a "hunting snaffle" with a running martingale, braided reins, and cavesson. Note that hunters wear plain browbands and that in appointments classes such as this one the reins and check straps are stitched to the bit.

Horse and rider in close accord over a hedge jump. Magyar Damsel, a gray mare owned by the Portaferry Farm in Camarillo, California, with Claudia Sacellary up.

The swinging gate indicates that this hunter had a light touch with his forelegs which will not be counted against him unless the competition is very close.

Richard Keller maintains a light contact with his reins as he takes Paper Roses owned by the Foxtail Farm of Portola Valley, California, over the red gate.

An experienced horseman always keeps his eye on the next fence, never on the one he is negotiating.

Because this fence is part of an "in-and-out" and because of the crossed bars which raise the height of the obstacle, China Doll, ridden by Pam Linn and owned by Marcus Rudnick of Bakersfield, California, is giving an extra strong spring.

A rider in an appointments class waits to have his hunter checked for soundness.

Correct hunting attire for a member of the field includes silk hat, white stock, "pink" coat with collar in hunt colors and hunt buttons with special insignia, fawn breeches, and black boots with mahogany tops. Ladies would wear derbies and black melton coats or "shadbelly" coats with silk hats, children and members of the hunt staff would wear velvet caps. However, recently many riders showing in Corinthian and appointments classes, both men and women, have taken to wearing velvet hunt caps. Appointments for the horse include sandwich cases and flasks, but these are optional.

The winner of the appointments class was the gray gelding Sutton Place, ridden by Champ Hough and owned by Mr. and Mrs. R. C. Zellerback of Menlo Park, California. He is shown negotiating the imitation stone wall in the Santa Barbara Arena.

Jumper Division

Of all the classes offered the classes for jumpers are probably the most popular with spectators. The main reason for this popularity is that the rules are simple and the spectator always knows why a horse is eliminated or why he wins the class. This is not true in classes for hunters where manners, way of going, and so forth count. Jumpers may be of any breed or height; mild unsoundness which does not constitute cruelty to the horse if jumped does not count against him. The only thing which counts is whether or not he clears an obstacle without committing a disobedience and within the time allowed. If the horse touches an obstacle with any point of his body behind the stifle (point where front of back legs joins the body) he is penalized with ½ a fault. Touching an obstacle with any point of his body in front of the stifle or with any part of the rider or his equipment means a penalty of 1 fault. One fault is also incurred if a jumping standard or wing is touched by rider or horse. If the obstacle, the wing, or the standard is knocked down there is a penalty of 4 faults. Placing a foot in a Liverpool Jump or any other type of jump which uses a ditch or water as one of its component parts, or the knocking down of the take-off bar of such a jump, is also penalized 4 points. The first disobedience (refusal, run out, losing forward motion at trot or canter, extra circle,) 3 faults, second disobedience 6 faults, third disobedience elimination. The rider who starts before the judge tells him to, or before a knocked-down obstacle has been reset, or who takes the wrong course, or fails to enter the ring within one minute of being called, or fails to cross the starting line within one minute of having entered the ring is eliminated. The foregoing table of faults is from the AHSA scoring table I. Table II used in Knockdown, Puissance, and Six Bar classes is the same except that touches are not penalized. In the High Jump class, a class in which there is only one jump starting at 4′6″ or 5′0″ and being raised after each horse in the class has had three tries at it, is scored in points instead of faults, two points given for clearing the obstacle, one point for an obstacle jumped but knocked down.

Jumpers are classified as "Green" or "Open" jumpers. A Green Jumper is a horse that has not won more than two first-place ribbons in the Jumper Division of a Regular Show after January 1st of its five-year-old year. An Open Jumper is a horse that is not restricted by its previous winnings.

Jumping courses are interesting, and experienced planning of such a course greatly enhances the attraction of the class and the test of the entries. The course must not be so easy that all or most of the horses in the class have a clean round, nor so hard that none or possibly only one or two succeed in taking it without a fault. For Green Jumpers the minimum height is 3'9"; there is no maximum except that in the first round (i.e., before the jumpoffs to decide the winners of ties) the jumps may not be higher than 4'. This applies only to the first class of the day. In "spread" jumps (those composed of one or more elements, all of which must be taken at one leap) the minimum height is 4' and the minimum spread 4'. These heights apply to the larger shows which qualify as "A" or "B" shows. For "C" shows the minimum height and spread for Green Jumpers is 3'6" and for local shows there is no minimum. For Open Jumpers in "A" and "B" shows, the minimum height is 4', and the spread 5'. For "C" shows the spread is 4', with no minimum at local shows. All modern courses require several changes of direction and fairly sharp turns. A great variety of obstacles is common, there being no limit except that certain types such as double cross poles are prohibited. The AHSA has many rules pertaining to the timing of the horses. When time counts, or when the various types of classes recommended or the distances between obstacles regarded as best play an important role, the spectators would profit by studying the Association's annual rule book, which is a complimentary gift to members.

George Morris, former member of the U.S. Olympic Equestrian Team, mounts his Green Jumper Four Seasons.

An example of beautiful form on the part of both rider and horse as George Morris and Four Winds negotiate a triple bar.

The jump crew stands ready but this horse, Winsted, owned by the Colony Farms, jumps clean. Notice the fleece cavesson, the "mud tail," and the standing martingale.

Since clearing the obstacle is all-important, many horses are trained to throw their hind legs very high.

Women also compete in jumper classes. This is Olive Van Alstyne on Irish Mick. Notice the dropped noseband, a type of equipment which has become very popular in the last few years.

In the class for Open Jumpers, McLain Street, owned by the Duffy Stables of Bedford Village, Connecticut, and trained and ridden by John Bell, clears a double. McLain Street is one of the champion Open Jumpers of the country.

The second time around, McLain Street took off roughly but nevertheless managed to jump clean, showing the value of long experience.

High Frontier, owned by Jack B. Ward of Ward Acres Farm, Ridgefield, Connecticut, is a truly great horse. He is out of a mare named Predominate by Wait-A-Bit and his own sire was an Irish-bred stallion named Fairforall. He was bred and foaled at the Ward Acres Farm. As a three-year-old he was raced (being too big to be raced as a two-year-old) and won his maiden race. He was retired as a three-year-old after this race and did not return to the track, Mr. Ward having changed his mind regarding the future career of this appealing, big, blaze-faced colt. At the age of five he made his appearance as a Green Working Hunter and for the next three years won fame in this division under the care and tutelage of his trainer, David Kelley. In his second year of showing, still qualifying as a Green Working Hunter, he was named Horse of the Year in this division. But both his trainer and his owner decided after the three years of showing in the hunter division that this great horse

should be in the jumper division where he might, in time, prove his worth as Olympic material. In this picture we see the now nine-year-old race horse, working hunter, and jumper, and can admire the fine conformation and development which has made him a champion.

HORSES SHOWN UNDER SADDLE ON THE FLAT

American Saddle, Five-Gaited Section

The Gaited Saddler must show the walk (animated and graceful), the trot (square, collected, and balanced, with the hocks carried well under), the canter (smooth, slow, straight on the track on both leads), the "slow gait" (slow, high, animated and not a slow rack), and the rack, which is a four-beat gait done at speed and in form. Those being considered for ribbons must show all gaits in both directions, and, unless time is a factor, the judge will usually ask all horses to change directions for all gaits. The American Saddler, both three- and five-gaited, is judged on manners, presence, quality, conformation, and performance.

No Saddle Horses may be shown in a simple snaffle, and breast-plates and martingales are prohibited (except in Fine Harness classes.) A special cut of English saddle suited to the position of the rider and the gaits of the horse is used. The suggested dress of the rider is as follows: for informal, morning and afternoon classes, jodphurs, coat, and hat in light blue, gray, or tan. Gaudy colors are not considered appropriate. In the evening, five-gaited riders wear dark blue or black jodphurs and a tuxedo-type coat of the same material with a black derby. Riders of three-gaited horses wear the same but with a silk hat.

Classes for Saddle Horses, both three- and five-gaited, may be divided as to age (Junior Saddle Horses being four years old and under) or in the regular Maiden, Novice and Limit classes. Junior Saddle Horses may be further divided into classes for three year olds and classes for four year olds. Other classifications include Ladies, Junior Exhibitors, Amateurs, Owners, or Amateur Owners to Ride. Open classes are open to any American Saddle Horses. It is these which carry the highest point score toward championships and other awards.

David Kelley, rider and trainer, on High Frontier, winner of this Open Jumper class. Here he shows his powerful spring as he clears the 4'6" spread jump by at least a foot.

Barbara Slaymaker rides Destiny's Genius at the "slow gait." Although most Saddlers in training for showing are too highly schooled and sensitive for other work, after they are retired they sometimes can be reschooled as pleasure horses and spend their later years on roads and trails.

Wild Wind of River Farm, Avon, Connecticut, at the rack.

The winning horse of this class was Moon Dancer owned by Betty Focht. Notice that his forearm is horizontal to the ground and the hock action matches it. The cannon is vertical, which means that the horse is reaching out well and that there is no danger of his cutting himself on the elbow.

This horse, also at the rack, is not quite so evenly cadenced and does not carry his head well.

In the three-gaited division, Extra Assignment shows the strength, squareness, and "reach" needed at the trot.

Daring Duke, owned by the River Farm, shows the qualities of finish and presence.

In this photograph it is easy to see the heavy pads and long toes worn by Saddlers to give them action and reach.

The rider is careful to maintain the even cadence and the steadiness as he lines up.

America's Carol, owned by a young man named Chip Ghen and ridden by Bobbie Stevens, is the winner of the class. On receiving the trophy Miss Stevens smiles delightedly and America's Carol says, "I told you I could do it!"

These are horses that are judged on their suitability as pleasure mounts on the bridle path. There are various types with special classes for each. These include Bridlepath Hacks, American Saddle Horse Type; Bridlepath Hacks, Hunter Type; English Pleasure and Pleasure Horses of specific breeds; and local Pleasure Horses limited to owners who live within a specified distance of the show in question. Here we see Dock Dinnocka, registered Morgan gelding, being shown in an English Pleasure class. He is owned by Stonecroft Farm of Dalton, Pennsylvania. In this class he will be asked to show a flat-footed walk, an easy trot, and a comfortable canter. He may be asked to go on a completely loose rein if the judge so desires, but he must also be willing to perform on a lightly stretched rein as shown here.

Sport Flash (sire Special Assignment, dam Sport Gossip) is a registered American Saddle Horse. Here we see him in a Bridlepath Hack class for horses of the American Saddle type. Holly Simpson, who owns and shows him, has shown him successfully also in Road Hack and Pleasure classes.

Tom Cat, a chestnut gelding owned by Thomas Troy, is also American Saddle bred. He is shown here by Lois T. Gillette; he has somewhat higher action that some of the other horses in this class, but it is not exaggerated action. Notice the light contact of the reins, a requirement in Bridlepath Hack classes, and the calmness of the horse.

Walking Horse Division

   The qualifying gaits of the Tennessee Walking Horse are the flat walk, which must be true and square with a cadenced head motion; the running walk, a smooth, gliding, overstepping four-square gait demonstrating stride and pronounced head motion; and the canter, smooth, slow, and straight. The horse may wear bell boots, but these are limited to a maximum of two inches at the heel and three and one-half inches at the bell in height, and may not weigh more than eight ounces. There have been instances of cruelty in which sharp points were introduced in the boots to cause the horse to have a flashier, faster gait at the running walk, and the AHSA rules state specifically that all boots must be smooth on the inside and that judges must be on the look-out for violations. Certainly the "Walkers" have developed such a tremendously strong gait that one wonders whether the original purpose of the breed, to provide an easy-gaited animal for the southern plantation owner who wanted to ride over planted areas in comfort, has not been lost sight of.

Blue Roan, a Tennessee Walker, shown at the running walk. (Photo by June Fallaw)

99

MORGANS UNDER SADDLE

The Morgan Horse is the only breed which takes its name from one foundation sire—namely, Justin Morgan. This little horse, only a pony in size, was best known for his tremendous stamina and for his versatility. He had tremendous muscular development with great shoulder angulation and depth. His disposition was good (though he is said to have hated small dogs) and he was not nervous or highstrung. Above all he had the power to pass along these characteristics. Some of today's Morgans greatly resemble their ancestor, while others, through selective breeding, have changed somewhat. The Morgan Horse Association and the American Horse Show Association alike are discouraging the tendency of some breeders to make the Morgan over into a Saddle Horse. For this reason the setting or gingering of tails, the adding of artificial hair to the manes or tails, and the use of boots, heavy pads, or heavy shoes are prohibited.

Recognizing the importance of the versatility of the Morgan, the AHSA suggests classes which will give these horses a chance to show their different aptitudes, though, unlike Justin Morgan, the same horse need not necessarily have the qualifications which would enable him to win in all these classes.

We have primarily the Pleasure Morgan and the Performance Morgan. The former again is divided into Pleasure Morgans under English tack and those wearing Western tack. The emphasis in these classes is the ability of the horse to give the rider a good ride, with manners and gait to count 60 per cent and conformation 40 per cent. Performance Morgans are also judged on presence and quality. Performance Harness Morgans (see that division in this book) are judged as are other harness classes and must conform to the judge's idea of a stylish harness horse. Combination Morgans are shown first hitched to a vehicle and then under saddle. Versatile Morgans are shown first driven, then ridden, and finally asked to take two obstacles not to exceed 3'. In the Western Division, Morgans may also be shown as Parade Horses, Trail Horses or Stock Horses and are judged according to the rules for those classes (see Western Division in this book). All Morgans shown as such must be registered with the Morgan Horse Association. The following pictures, taken at the Farmington Show, show the two main types of Morgans, the Pleasure Morgans and the Performance Morgans. Harness Morgans will be found in Chapter Three.

Pleasure Morgans on the track at the trot. Riders wear saddle horse outfits; horses are sturdy but not "flashy."

Jane D. Raucher shows Lady Roxana
whose calmness and alertness pleased
the judges . . .

. . . who later presented her with the
trophy.

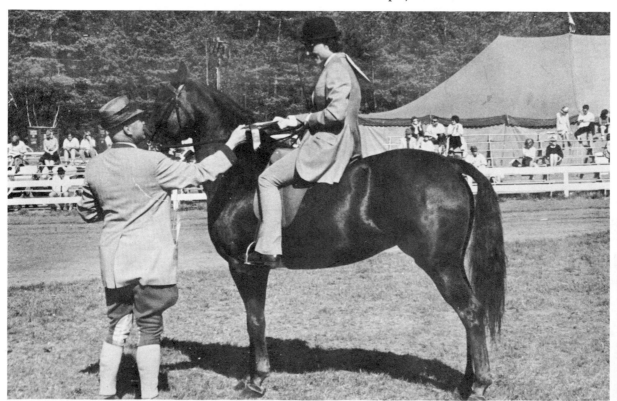

Performance Morgans

Kerry Dancer, owned by the Waseeka
Farm, is an example of a "Performance Morgan."

The judge inspects the entries in a "Performance Morgans Under Fifteen Hands" category . . .

. . . and selects Windcrest Show Girl, a chestnut mare, 14:3, eight years old owned by Helen Stofer of Norwich, New York.

HORSES SHOWN IN WESTERN TACK

In addition to special classes for horses of specific breeds, there are three types of horses shown in the performance classes in the Western Division. These are Pleasure Horses, Trail Horses, and Stock Horses. Parade Horses are also part of this division but are not judged as working horses, the costume, tack, and "parade type" of appearance being the deciding factors.

Horses may be of any breed or combination of breeds and must be 14:1 hands or over. They must be serviceably sound and in good condition, but what in a hunter class would be called "honorable scars" are permitted. In this division stallions are permitted in classes limited to Ladies to Ride and Juniors. The tack used is specifically described. In the trail and pleasure classes, entries are shown in a stock saddle, a standard Western bit without joints, or a curb, halfbreed or spade bit, but no bosal or cavesson type noseband is permitted. The chin strap must be of leather without any wire, chain or metal or any rawhide device on it to make it more severe. Tiedowns, chokes, and martingales are prohibited. The headstall of the bridle may be either the "one-eared" type or the type with a browband. If split reins are used no hobbles are required, but if closed reins are used hobbles must be carried. The bridle and saddle may be decorated with silver, but this does not add points. In the stock horse classes the same limitations as to tack applies, but in some stock horse classes a jaquima (a type of hackamore) is worn instead of a bridle.

Riders must be in Western dress with Western hats, chaps and cowboy boots and must carry a rope or reata. The type of shirt to be worn is not designated and one sees all types of sweaters from dark with indian motif figures to pale pink cable-stitch angora. The neatest and most popular for women seems to be a perfectly starched plain white blouse with either a narrow tie or a silk choker.

Arabians compete against other breeds such as stock, trail or pleasure horses and also against each other in classes limited to others of their breed. Here we see an example of an Arabian in Western tack at the walk. Notice the extreme aimiability of his expression as well as his keen alertness, both being innate characteristics of a breed whose members were kept in the tents of their masters to act as watchdogs. (Photo by June Fallaw)

Arabian

A class of Western Pleasure Horses lines up before the judge. The horses stand naturally and calmly with the exception of the third horse from the right which has been taught to stretch.

Trail and Pleasure Horses are shown at the walk, jog, trot, and lope. The rider must carry the reins in one hand with his fingers around the reins and both hands must be held clear of the saddle at all times. The horse must work on a reasonably loose rein without undue restraint. Special emphasis is placed on the walk, for these horses must carry their riders over rough ground and up and down steep inclines at this gait. The lope, from the point of view of comfort to the rider, is also important.

Horses are shown at all gaits in both directions and must show the correct lead at the lope.

This is a dun gelding owned by Mr.
and Mrs. Robert G. Haley of Ventura,
California. His calmness and obedi-
ence pleased the judge.

Later he was called out of line to be
pinned first. Molly's Man is not a
pampered darling kept just for showing. He has years of service behind
him as shown by the scar from a bad
wire-cut on his chest. He is a registered
Quarter Horse, seven years old, and
has been one of the top winners of
the state in both Pleasure and Trail
Horse seven years old, and has been
one of the top winners of the state in
both Pleasure and Trail Horse classes.
He is shown by Virginia Haley, aged
thirteen.

The second classification of the Western performance horse is the Trail Horse.

In addition to showing the gaits in both directions the Trail Horse is put through certain tests to demonstrate his usefulness on the trail. The first of these is his willingness to cooperate with the rider when a gate must be opened . . .

. . . and closed again. Notice that the rider completes the operation without letting go of the gate with her right hand. As she pushes it to, the horse will step sideways towards it, enabling her to latch it. This is Sage Mo, ridden by Brennie Grant of Woodside, California.

Cynthia Willis on Casino, who, following the gate test, lopes in a small circle.

The next test is to show the horse's willingness to cross strange and perhaps terrifying objects which may be encountered. This is a difficult test, for all horses are, by inheritance, afraid of stepping on something which might hurt their feet. The obstacle chosen for this test is a number of tires, some painted white, laid down on the ground, with the rims touching and decorated with brush. Hey Boy, owned by Mr. and Mrs. C. W. Bertler and ridden by Ted Ford, steps calmly but attentively through the tires.

The Trail Horse must back willingly, quietly, and exactly as the rider demands. Here you see a difficult backing test. The horse is backed into the pen and must then weave around, still backing, between the slender staves . . .

. . . until he backs out into the clear again.

This is Pancho, owned and ridden by Don B. Kilbourne, of Santa Ynez, California.

Bridges are commonplace on the tra[...]
and often terrifying.

Having negotiated the bridge the
horse shows his calmness in cantering
a figure eight. Note the rider in formal
hunting attire watching from the
adjoining schooling area.

The final test is to walk over a row
of crossed poles.

The tests given the stock horse are designed to demonstrate its training and ability in working stock. The judge decides on the exact pattern of figures which he would like executed and explains them to the class before the competition begins.

The test usually begins with a figure eight executed at the lope. Starting on a circle to the left . . .

. . . the rider completes the circle, then crosses through the center . . .

116

. . . executes a flying change and continues on a circle to the right. The figure eight is ridden several times after which . . .

. . . the rider lopes at speed but still on a loose rein. The horse must appear to be under control even when going fast. Notice that the horse is wearing not a bridle but a "jaquima" (a bitless bridle). Jaquima classes are limited to five-year-old animals that have never been shown in a bridle.

At a designated point the horse is brought to a halt. He must bring his legs in under him in stopping and his head should be in a natural position.

The horse is now asked to turn on his hindquarters, a half turn in each direction.

At this point he may be required to back, or this test may be given later. This horse will be penalized for opening his mouth unduly in backing, a common fault in horses whose training has been rushed.

Stock horses are judged on a basis of 100 points for a perfect score, rein work as described to count 50 points, conformation 20 points, manners 20 points, and appointments 10 points. In addition, obvious faults in performance, an undue switching of the tail, nervous throwing of the head, or any halt or hesitation indicating that the horse is anticipating his signals, are penalized. Stock horse classes may be divided as follows: Green Stock Horses (those which have never been shown before January 1st of the current year), Lightweight (850–1100 lbs.), and Heavyweight (over 1100 lbs.). There are also classes for Junior riders, in which particular attention is paid to the lightness of the hands of the riders, Ladies to Ride classes (stallions may not be used in either of the last mentioned classes) and Jaquima classes.

A flying start from the halt and the contestant lopes back at speed to the other end of the arena where the same tests are executed.

He now gallops half the length of the
arena and halts . . .

. . . makes a quarter turn on the haunches, and walks quietly forward to
the judge.

Notice how well Snippy Reed, owned by Richard Downing balances himself on the figure eight, his hindlegs following on the track of his front legs.

On small circles the horse must carry his inside hindleg well under him.

121

This horse would not be considered to be extending himself sufficiently on the lope down the arena.

Top Kick, ridden by Hugh McHugh shows how a well-trained horse stops. The head is brought in to the chest but the profile is still vertical and the neck flexes well at the poll. The horse's mouth is closed; the horse comes to a halt with all four feet on the ground.

This horse keeps his mouth closed but throws his head up.

This horse is obviously lacking in training or else the bit is too severe and rider's hands too heavy. Notice the wide open mouth.

Miss Jeanie Buck, owned by Robert J. Runnings and ridden by Richard Smith, backs correctly. Again the poll is flexed, the profile vertical, the mouth soft and yielding, and the horse steps back calmly.

This horse is resisting the rider by bracing his jaw and opening his mouth.

Appaloosa Horse Division

The Appaloosa is a color breed. Horses eligible for registry must conform to the color and marking patterns as set up by the Appaloosa Horse Association. The dark spots are detectable by feel as well as visually. The breed is also characterized by longitudinal white stripes on the hoofs and by white around the iris of the eye. Appaloosas may be as small as 14 hands and most are under 15:3, and weights run from 950 to 1175 pounds. In addition to being well conformed with strong but not common lines, the "ideal Appaloosa" should have a deep but not excessively wide chest, well-defined withers, and good length and slope of pastern, shoulder, and hip. The Indians claimed that horses and ponies of this marking had the most stamina and were far stronger for size and weight than were animals of other colors. Appaloosas may be shown in Western classes of all kinds under Western tack, in Bridlepath Hack and Trail, Jumping, and other classes under English tack as well as to special classes limited to horses of their breed which include racing and gymkhana-type events. They may also compete in open performance classes of all kinds. The author was interested to find a fine Appaloosa hunter on the hunting fields of Ireland. There it was known as a "colored" horse and the owner was interested to learn of the popularity of this breed in America. Pictures of early Spanish horses include many Appaloosas and it is no doubt from the horses imported by the Spanish explorers that we owe the introduction of the Appaloosa to the New World.

In the foreground an Appaloosa with the characteristic "blanket" type of markings, i.e., mottled forehand and spotted quarters. Behind can be seen a horse with spotted forehand. (Photo by June Fallaw)

Special event class of Appaloosas. (Photo by June Fallaw)

Parade Horse

The Parade Horse must be a beautiful and stylish animal displaying refinement, and personality and presenting an eye-appealing picture of a matched and costumed horse and rider. He is shown at two gaits, the animated walk which must be a four-beat, graceful movement, not a jog trot, and slow enough to differentiate it from the "Parade Gait." The latter is a true, square, high-prancing gait; a five-mile-an-hour gait (the average walk of other types is four miles an hour, the trot is from eight to nine miles an hour). Such a gait is similar to a "Spanish Walk" or a "Spanish Trot" in which there is a distinct period of suspension as the legs are lifted in turn. The rider must wear Mexican, Spanish or Western dress, silver trimmed, with matching appointments, saddle, and briddle. The horse may be any color, and a mare, gelding or stallion, and though a high tail may be carried it must be a natural tail and not one that has been artificially "set." A tail switch is permitted but no boots, martingales, etc. Parade Horses are judged as follows: performance, manners, and conformation, 75 per cent; appointments of horse and rider, 25 per cent.

The silver-trimmed saddle and appointments of this exhibitor as well as his intricately embroided costume are both heavy and costly. (Photo by June Fallaw)

127

At the Parade Gait a beautifully trained Palomino shows a well-carried head
and good hock as well as knee action.
Horses must show both gaits in both
directions. (Photo by June Fallaw)

PONIES UNDER SADDLE

Pony Hunters are judged as are regular hunters. Wherever possible they take an outside course with the same types of jumps as the horses but set at heights according to the size of the pony. Ponies not exceeding 15 hands jump 2′6″; ponies over 13 but not exceeding 15:2 jump 3′.

In shows where the pony classes are large and the variation in size ranges from miniature to large, the classes may be divided three ways: ponies not exceeding 11:2 hands to jump 2′, over 11:2 and not to exceed 13 hands to jump 2′6″, and large ponies 3′. Ponies may be classified as Conformation and Working and may be further divided, as are hunters, into Maiden, Novice, Limit, Green, Regular and Qualified. When being judged on the flat the first four of the above classifications are not required to gallop on. Hunter ponies are judged over fences on manners, way of going, style of jumping, and pace, light ticks that do not displace the obstacle not to count. Scoring is the same as in the Hunter Division. (See Chapter Three).

A Pony Hunter class in the assembly area outside the hunt course at Farmington. On the bulletin board, which is being checked by a rider on a large pony, are charts of the courses.

129

There is just time before the class
is called for a mother to take a sticky
pony over a fence or so in hopes that
this last-minute schooling will make
him more willing under the less com-
petent hands of his young rider.

Gigi Bowen takes Criban Dart around the course. Dart is a chestnut gelding, 12 hands, seven years old. Gigi is attentively looking ahead, as she should.

Gail Hulick on Muffin Man, a roan gelding eight-year-old, 12:1½ hands, present the ideal picture of the Pony Club, a "happy child on a happy pony."

Between jumps the ponies move out at a regulation hunting pace. Abnormal speed is penalized but the pony should go fast enough to keep up to hounds when they are running on a line.

In Chapter 2 of this book you saw a picture of Campbell Kid stripped. Here you see him and his owner Robert Stearns of Irvington, New York, negotiating a brush jump in a thoroughly workmanlike manner.

In California, Scott McClurg takes his versatile little mount, Stoately Wells Cargo, owned by Mrs. David Wells, around a hunt course set up in the covered area. (Photo by George Axt)

Outside the ring Leslie Brandt anxiously waits with her pony Chaff to find out whether or not she will be called back as one of the winners. Leslie is wearing formal hunt livery but with a "choker" instead of a stock.

A group of large Pony Hunters being judged under saddle on the flat at Farmington. They will be asked to walk trot and canter, and if Qualified or Regular Ponies, to gallop on.

In the large pony division, Meta Boy-kin, on Mastercraft, flies over a post and rail. (Freudy Photos)

Miss Susan Cullman on Heaven Sent, her five-year-old Pony Hunter, 14:1 hands. Again we see the jump set up for Pony Hunters is an extension of the higher bars set for full-sized hunters. Post and rails are among the most common type of obstacle and more difficult than they appear, for many horses and ponies get careless over them. (Carl Klein photo)

Chinchilla, another example of a beautifully made Large Pony Hunter. He is being shown by John Watson. (Freudy Photos)

Pony Jumpers

Specifications, scoring, and classification of Pony Jumpers follow along the same lines as those for jumpers in the horse division. The heights are the same as for Pony Hunters, the only exception being that in case of a tie the jumps may be raised gradually to a maximum of 9″ in each division. If, after jumping the course at the maximum height allowed, there is still a tie, the contenders will divide the prize money and the points. Championships are decided on a basis of points won previously throughout the jumper section of that show. Since there are fewer classes for Hunter and Jumper Ponies than there are for horses it is quite usual to see the same ponies competing in both divisions.

Stoatley Wells Cargo makes certain of clearing the obstacle in a jumper class. Such form over a jump in a Pony Hunter Class would be penalized but pony jumpers are scored only on actual faults incurred in jumping. When Cargo finds himself showing as a Hunter he jumps quite differently. (See Chapter 3.) (Photo by June Fallaw)

137

Bantam, dam Dark Sprite (registered Welsh), sire unknown was Champion Small Pony at the Maryland Pony Show, 1962, at the National Show (Madison Square Garden) 1963, and at Fairfield, in 1964. (Freudy Photos)

Welsh Pony Under Saddle

The Welsh Mountain Pony is one of the most versatile of ponies. In the list of recommended performance classes we find Welsh Pleasure Ponies, English Equipment; and Welsh Pleasure Ponies, Western Equipment; Welsh Trail Ponies, English or Western Equipment; Welsh Pleasure Driving Ponies to be shown to suitable two-or four-wheeled vehicle; Welsh Roadster Ponies driven to a bike; and Welsh Roadster Ponies under saddle. There are also classes for Welsh Formal Driving Ponies, including classes for pairs of ponies driven abreast and tandem. Welsh ponies are also very popular in the Pony Hunter divisions, the Pony Jumper, and Equitation classes both on the flat and over jumps. Unlike the Shetland, which started as a child's pony and has been turned into something quite different, the highly bred Welsh Show Pony is probably the best pony of all to be a child's companion and servant.

Welsh Ponies at the trot in an English Pleasure class.

Welsh Ponies at the canter, English Pleasure.

Stoatley Wells Cargo, owned by Mrs. David Wells of Santa Barbara, California, is shown being presented with the trophy in a Western Pleasure Class for Welsh Ponies. His rider, Master Scott McClurg, aged nine, also shows him in English Pleasure, Roadster, Jumping, and Equitation classes. (Photo by June Fallaw)

Seren Cookie, another Welsh pony belonging to Mrs. Wells, is shown by young Master McClurg in an English Pleasure class. (Photo by George Axt)

Costume classes are not as common as some, but aimiable Wells Cargo is glad to pose as a circus pony when needed in that capacity.

HARNESS DIVISION

Although strictly speaking the Harness division should refer only to the so-called Fine Harness horses and harness ponies, I have included in this division all horses and ponies that are shown to a suitable vehicle. This includes Fine Harness, Roadster, and Morgan in the Horse Division. In the Pony Division are Hackney, Harness with Long Mane and Tail, Roadster, Pony, Welsh, and Shetland. In each division the type of vehicle is specified in the rules laid down by the AHSA as well as all the clothes to be worn by the exhibitor. Entries are shown at the walk and trot in both directions, while some are also expected to show both the Park Trot and to trot at speed. After working together entries are lined up and an attendant usually stands at their heads while the judge walks along the line. A selected six or eight horses are then asked to take the track again and are judged once more at the different gaits in both directions. Harness classes bring to mind the days when a fast, stylish, well-mannered horse was as desirable and as much a status symbol as today's Mercedes Benz.

A Fine Harness entry with three grooms to help is prepared for entering the ring.

Fine Harness Horse

The Fine Harness horse is a Five-Gaited American Saddle Horse with long mane and undocked tail shown to an appropriate vehicle, preferably a small buggy with four wire wheels (viceroy). Light harness and a snaffle bit with an overhead check are required. The qualifying gaits are an animated graceful walk and an animated Park Trot. Extreme speed is penalized but high, stylish action is desirable. The Fine Harness horse must stand quietly but is not required to back. He may be judged on quality, presence, performance, conformation, finish, and manners, though not all of these qualities are taken into consideration in every class for Fine Harness horses.

A Fine Harness horse at the Park Trot. (Photo by June Fallaw)

143

This is an unusual color for a Fine Harness horse, chestnuts and bays being the preferred colors. (Photo by June Fallaw)

Harness Pony

The Harness Pony is distinguished from the *Small Hackney Pony* in that he wears a long mane and tail. Harness Ponies are limited in size to 12:2 hands. They are required to show a Park Trot and then are asked to take a smarter trot (but still not a racing trot) on the command "Show your pony." Most Harness Ponies are small Hackneys. However, if they show in the Harness Pony Division they may not show in the small Hackney Division.

A Class of Harness Ponies lined up for judging.

Park trot with good knee and hock action. Mizpah's Echo, owned by Mrs. Joseph Donato.

Show your pony! Little Joe, owned by Webster Knight II of Providence, Rhode Island, steps out.

The winner of the class was Diamond Victory, owned by the Brookmont Farms. This pony with long mane and tail is one of the most outstanding Harness Ponies in competition in the East.

Hackney Pony

The maximum height for Hackney Ponies is 14:2 hands. Classes are often divided into small and large divisions, *i.e.,* classes for ponies 13 hands and under, and those for ponies that exceed 13 hands but do not exceed 14:2. They may also be shown in pairs abreast and tandem. A special class for Hackneys is called "Collection of Three Hackney Ponies"; they are shown either in single harness or as a pair and as a single harness pony. Each team enters the ring and gives a solo performance, and is judged on performance as a unit with proper distance between vehicles, uniformity and quality to count.

Sir Pripe, driven by Mrs. David Wells of Santa Barbara, shows beautiful action.

Morgan Horses are shown in harness to an appropriate four-wheeled vehicle at an animated walk and an animated trot. They are judged on performance, quality, presence, manners, and suitability as a stylish harness horse, these to total 60 per cent, type and conformation to total 40 per cent. Drivers wear a business suit and felt hat or other suitable headgear. Classes may be divided as to age (Junior Morgans being those under five years), height, or experience.

The judge passes down the line of Morgans in harness. Since the young mare nearest the camera has been judged and seems restless, the driver moves her out to circle once and come back to position.

Applevale Magician, a three-year-old brown Morgan stallion, shows the natural, ground-covering trot required in Morgan classes.

Winner of the class is Wild Orchid
of Wasseeka Farm, owned by Mrs.
D. D. Power.

Morgans are much calmer in disposition than are the high-spirited little
harness ponies and the Fine Harness
horses. Notice how quietly this Morgan leaves the ring after the class
is over.

Pony Roadster

Roadsters are generally Standardbred horses though they are not required to be registered in the Standardbred registry. There are two types: those which are shown to a "bike" and those shown to a wagon. Occasionally there may be horses suitable to be shown to either one or the other, but generally speaking the Roadster shown to a wagon is a larger animal than the other. In any case he must carry a natural mane and tail and have good conformation. He is required to show the walk and three phases of the trot; the jog trot, the fast road gait, and the full speed or racing trot. At all these gaits he must show good flexibility of hocks and knees and straight true action. Roadsters may also be shown under saddle (English) and the same gaits are required. Under saddle and to bike, exhibitors wear stable silks, when shown to a wagon they wear a business suit and suitable hat.

Spitfire, owned by Dr. Howard G. Roberts and driven by Charles Count, was winner of the $500 Roadster Championship, shown to bike at the California State Fair. (Photo by June Fallaw)

On the command "Drive on!" Roadsters show what they can do.

Pony Roadsters are judged as are the ordinary roadsters being shown either to a bike or a wagon, as the class demands. Riders wear stable silks when shown to a bike. Classes may be divided into large or small divisions with no specification as to breed, or they may be limited to ponies of specified breeds.

Men, women, or children may show in Roadster Pony classes. Here we see a boy whose legs are just long enough to permit him to get his feet into the "stirrups" of the bike driving with confidence in a crowded class at the Farmington Show.

An expert driver steadies a nervous
entry.

In event of a mishap to the harness,
repairs may be made in the ring.

On the command "Show your ponies!"
the entry lengthens his stride. This is
Bandleader, owned and driven by
Mrs. Wilson Fox of Waterford,
Connecticut.

A group of Shetland Roadsters "comin 'round the bend" at speed.

The lovely chestnut Shetland stallion shown in Chapter Two shows what he can do in harness.

Imperial Stoatley Acorn, Welsh Mountain Pony driven by Mrs. David Wells, is winner for the third year in the Roadster class. (Photo by Cosner)

Welsh ponies may also be shown in harness as "Welsh Pleasure Driving Ponies." Either a two- or a four-wheeled vehicle is considered appropriate, but not a viceroy or fine harness rig. They must stand quietly and back readily and are not required to show speed at the trot. This is Seren Tanio being driven by Mrs. David Wells. (Photo by June Fallaw)

156

4.
Equitation Classes

EQUITATION ON THE FLAT

Equitation classes are those in which it is the performance of the rider alone which is judged. There are three divisions of Equitation classes on the flat requiring three different types of seat; these are the Hunter Seat Section, the Saddle Seat Section, and the Western Section. There is also the "lead line" class for those riders six years old and under. In some cases a class which combines more than one type of seat may be held and the judge must judge it accordingly.

Riders competing in Equitation classes are often divided as to age or as to experience thus we have "Maiden" classes for riders who have never won a blue ribbon at a recognized show, "Novice" classes for those who have not won more than three blue ribbons, and "Limit" classes for those who have not won more than six. If a rider shows in more than one section, ribbons won in the "Hunter Seat" section do not affect his status in the "Saddle" or "Stock" (Western) seat classes. However in the Hunter Seat section, ribbons won on the flat do affect the classification of the rider when he competes over jumps, but those won over jumps do not affect his classification in the classes on the flat. Ribbons won in lead line classes or in those which do not require that the rider go at all gaits do not count in future classification. Ribbons won in camp or school shows which are not recognized by the AHSA do not count either.

Riders may also be divided according to age. It is up to the Horse Show Committee how these classes are divided, and this depends again on the number of entries. The most usual is to hold classes for Juniors who have not reached their fourteenth birthday and for those who have passed fourteen but have not reached their eighteenth bithday. The birthday of any rider is considered to be December 31st of any given year; thus he maintains whatever age he was on the 1st of January of the current season.

Since the performance of the horse does not count, whatever type horse is suitable in type and training to the type of riding being performed is used. Stallions are prohibited in all classes. However, the choice of a suitable horse for the rider showing in any of the three divisions is all-important. If he is to be shown over jumps he must jump willingly and smoothly. If he is to be shown on the flat he must have smooth gaits and an alert appearance, and above all he must have presence and the ability to "catch the judges eye" and to make the rider look well.

The AHSA gives detailed description of what it considers a good basic position in all three divisions, though it does not specify the position over jumps. It also lists the types of tests which may be asked in the different contests for riders of various ages and qualifications in all three divisions.

Lead Line Class

Many future champions make their initial appearance in the horse show arena in a lead line class. The AHSA does not list such classes in its rule book but over the years the rules have become standardized. Entries are usually boys or girls between the ages of four and six, though occasionally a younger child appears in the ring. The young hopefuls may wear any type of dress they consider suitable and ride any type of pony. The youngster must be led by an adult or older child on foot. (Occasionally one finds classes in which the rider may be led by a mounted rider. In such classes the competitors are asked to trot as well as walk.) The rider is judged on position only at the walk and while the pony is standing. No questions are asked by the judges, but the riders are usually asked to walk in both directions. It has become customary for the Show Committee to provide as many ribbons as there are entries, the duplications being in the ribbons of lowest value. Thus if six ribbons are being awarded there will be enough sixth ribbons (green) to go around; if eight, there will be extra eighth (brown) ribbons so that no young rider leaves the ring feeling that he has failed.

Master Robert G. Becker, wearing formal hunting attire, is led by his mother who judging by her costume, favors the saddle seat.

Pixie Gillies, age five on her gray pony Severn Thistle enters the ring and takes the track to the left. Pixie sits very straight and has her legs well under her. She is wearing what would be called "rat catcher" or "hacking" clothes. Her pony, as well as the other ponies in this class, would be classified as a "Pet Pony."

Master Wirsul of Bloomfield, Connecticut, is comfortable in cowboy attire. His pony is named "Jimmy" and James and his brother and sister, Robert and Nancy, take complete care of him. Note that James rides the Western seat with his reins in one hand and an almost straight leg.

Outside the smaller ring at Farmington, which is reserved for Model and Equitation classes, two young competitors chat aimably while waiting for their class to be called. Notice the letter "E" above the number 122 on the back of the rider on the right. This tells the spectator that it is an Equitation class, not a Performance class and that the rider, not the horse, is being judged. The horses with braided tails show that they are hunters, not Saddlers, and the riders wear hunt caps and high boots, so the spectator also knows without being told that these young young ladies are competing for a "hunter seat" trophy.

Dale Ann Pace, age five, was the winner of the class. She is riding her gentle spotted gelding, Peter Pan. Dale is shown trotting out of the ring, with her silver trophy.

While the aforementioned contestants wait for their class, a class in which riders of both hunter and saddle seat is taking place. The two riders in the foreground are saddle seat riders while the boy on the gray wearing the top boots is obviously hunter seat.

In the "hunter seat" the rider sits in the middle of the saddle, with the weight on the buttock points, but not on the buttocks. Stirrup leathers must hang vertical to the ground, with the point of toe directly under point of knee, a straight line running from the rider's ankle through his hip bone to his ear, except when in motion, when the upper body is carried slightly forward matching the forward motion of the horse. Hands are never flat but relaxed, slightly ahead of the pommel of the saddle and separated, the reins being held in both hands. In both seats the heels are depressed but, as shown in this picture, the hunter seat requires that the ankle be bent in slightly, and the toes of the rider point slightly out in a natural position. As can be seen by comparing the girl's foot position with that of the young man behind her, who is riding a "saddle seat," in the latter the feet are nearly flat and exactly parallel to the horse.

Here is an example of the accepted saddle seat at a canter. Notice that the rider sits somewhat farther back and carries his weight to the rear rather than forward as in the previous picture of the hunter seat. Note, too, that the stirrup leathers are pushed forward with the rider's toe being somewhat ahead of the point of his knee.

If a horse or pony gets out of hand in an Equitation class, the Ring Master must bring it in to the center of the ring at once and the judges then decide whether the competitor shall leave the ring or stay lined up until the class is judged.

Stock Seat Division

Judging of Stock Seat Equitation classes takes into consideration the position of the rider and his knowledge of the use of his aids, the performance of the horse, the appointment of horse and rider, and the suitability of horse to rider. Riders are required to mount and dismount and to back as well as to perform the ordinary routine of the stock horse. Since one of the requirements is that the saddle must be exactly the right size for the rider, competitors are not required to change horses even in open and championship classes.

In the accepted standard for the Stock Seat, the rider sits in the middle of the saddle with a straight back and head up. Legs may either be pushed a little forward with a straight knee or may be slightly bent with the foot under the rider, but in either case the heel must be lower than the toe, the weight of the rider must rest on the ball of the foot, and the rider must be completely relaxed. Arms hang straight, with the left hand, which carries the reins, bent at the elbows, the right hand resting on the thigh. The rider must sit the jog trot and be down in the saddle at the canter. The horse must work off his haunches with his head in a straight line with his body, he must be quick and willing as well as flexible in his movements and always be in perfect balance. The Western horse is trained to obey the neck rein and not to go on the bit, so the reins are not stretched as is the case in the hunter and saddle seats. As in all equitation contests, the signals that the rider gives his horse must be imperceptible. Classes may be divided according to age (those under eleven, those from eleven to fourteen and those fourteen to eighteen) or experience (Maiden, Novice and Limit). Championships are never awarded on points won in previous classes but are ridden off, the contestants being those who have won red or blue ribbons in at least one other open class in the show.

The Stock Seat at the jog. This bridle rein is fitted with a romal (added strip of leather to which the two reins are stitched) must be carried on the off side. With such a rein the rider must keep his hand around the reins without putting a finger in between as is allowed with split reins. Also in using split reins the ends must be carried on the near side. (Photo by June Fallaw)

A pretty teenager on a well-built stock horse wins a championship ribbon and trophy in Equitation. Championship ribbons consist of three long streamers, one blue, one red, and one yellow. Reserve championship ribbons are red, yellow, and white. (Photo by June Fallaw)

The Stock Seat at the lope. This bridle also has a romal. The rider may hold the end of it in his right hand to keep it from swinging, but that hand must be no less than 14″ from his other hand. With split reins the rider carries his right hand on his thigh. (Photo by June Fallaw)

Horsemanship over Jumps

In this division the rider is judged on his position, control, and knowledge of the use of the aids over a course of jumps. The judging of these classes, as with the other Equitation classes, is most difficult for a person with an untrained eye to understand. Since there are several acceptable variations in what is considered the best position to assume in order to make it as easy as possible for a horse to negotiate an obstacle, the AHSA does not define the seat over jumps. However, certain basic rules are adhered to by all authorities. These are as follows: the rider must not interefer with his horse by so distributing his weight that it handicaps the horse; he must not restrict the use of the horse's head in balancing itself; he must not lose contact and consequently communication with his horse by riding with reins that are very loose and flapping; he must not disturb the horse by rough or uncadenced use of the legs; he must not look down either at the ground or at the jump that he is in the process of taking, rather his head must be up and his eyes on the next obstacle in the course. At all times the rider's body must follow the movements of the horse, and his legs from the crotch to half way down the calf must maintain a light contact. As in the hunter seat on the flat, the knees are well bent, the stirrup leather vertical to the ground, the rider's toe in line with his knee, the heel depressed and the ankle bone bent slightly in. The hands follow the movement of the horse's head. It must be apparent to the judge that the rider is controlling the horse and directing both its direction and its speed. Rider and horse together must present a harmonious picture of willing cooperation at all times. Regarding the heights of jumps, Maiden, Novice, Limit, and riders under fourteen years of age take obstacles whose height does not exceed 3'. In Open classes and Medal classes the jumps may not exceed 3'6". Any or all contestants may be called back to show at the walk, trot, and canter at the judge's discretion.

Miss Sherri Weinstein on Sputnik shows good form in a Horsemanship over Jumps class for riders under fourteen. Legs, seat, back, and head all excellent. Her hands could have been a little lower and away from the neck but this is not to be expected in a class for riders of her age. (Freudy Photos)

Park Holland III shows how the hands should be. Notice the straight line which runs from the rider's elbow, along his forearm, and along the lightly stretched rein to the bit. He is riding Count Roe, an ideal type of mount for this kind of competition.

Miss Abigail Erdmann on Mr. Crisp has her eyes fixed on the next jump which requires a change of direction. The reason for this rule is that if the horse must be turned sharply on landing the rider must prepare him for the turn while he is in mid-air. This she does by the correct use of her aids, especially the distribution of her weight. (Photo by Budd)

Specific Equitation Classes

In addition to the ordinary Equitation and Horsemanship over Jumps classes described above, there are a few Specific classes. These classes follow a specified routine in all shows throughout the country, and to include them a show must have special permission from the AHSA. Riders qualify by winning a stated number of blue ribbons in their locale during any one season. Those who qualify may then compete in Madison Square Garden in November of that year. Specific classes to which these rules pertain include the ASPCA (MacClay) Class, the USET Equitation Class, and the AHSA Medal Classes for Hunter, Saddle, and Stock Seat riders.

Miss Lane Schulz, riding her horse First Impression, was the winner of the Maclay Trophy (ASPCA) in 1964. (Photo Courtesy Lane Schulz)

Miss Randi Stuart receiving the Trophy and championship ribbon in Madison Square Garden as winner of the AHSA Medal Class Saddle Seat. (Carl Klein photo)

James (Jim) Kohn on Stonehedge, won the AHSA Medal, Hunter Seat Trophy, at Madison Square Garden. Jim also placed reserve in the ASPCA behind Miss Schulz. In this picture Jim displays a perfect example of seat and hands over fences. (Photo by Budd)

5.

Exhibitions

Some of the larger horse shows include exhibitions of various types in their programs. These are a great drawing card, especially for those in the audience who may not have friends among the exhibitors and so not be particularly interested in one division or another. For many years the Royal Canadian Mounted Police put on their famous "Musical Ride" at Madison Square Garden. The beautiful Lipizzaner Stallions have also appeared there, as well as members of the Cadre Noire, the French riding team. The exhibitions are not always equestrian; an exhibition of the training and work of Scottish sheep dogs was one such popular feature which was included in the program of the Santa Barbara National Show. In addition, they had an exhibition of old carriages which were driven in each evening and taken around the arena once or twice while the ring was being cleared of jumps, and two other good exhibitions, the six-horse hitch of Clydesdales pulling a red beer wagon, and the dramatic reenactment of how a fire was handled, using an old-time hand-drawn hose cart and a fire engine pulled by three galloping fire horses. Pictures of these three exhibitions follow.

PARADE OF EARLY VEHICLES

One of the most interesting of the exhibitions which were part of the Santa Barbara Show was its collection of old vehicles. Pictures of two of these, the Drummer's Wagon and the Sailor's Wagon are shown in Chapter One of this book, as they were displayed outside the main arena. The first of these was driven from place to place by the itinerent salesman who thus displayed his wares to farmers and others. The Sailor's Wagon, used for both driving and showing, was a light vehicle quite often carried aboard ship so that, in port, its owner could have suitable transportation by

172

hiring a horse from the local livery stable. At every evening performance the Metlox Pottery Company sent a group of their vehicles into the ring hitched to suitable horses and with appropriately dressed passengers in each.

We see here the brougham (pronounced broom,) one of the most elaborate and beautiful vehicles in the collection. It was in such vehicles as these that socialites of Boston, Philadelphia, New York, and other cities drove to tea, to the opera, and to balls. The matched Hackney horses with their docked tails are in character as is their silver-trimmed patent leather harness. See the monograms on the blinders of the bridle. The vehicle has silver lamps and silver fittings inside. It has a luxurious mulberry satin lining, a covered foot step, and shades to cut out sun or rain. (Photo by June Fallaw)

For country calls, the lady's basket phaeton was popular. The rumble seat at the back was for a liveried attendent who held the horse's head when the owner mounted; the attendent then climbed in behind to be ready if needed to carry luggage, open gates, etc. In an emergency, the lady could also pass the reins back to him. This Phaeton was made by A. T. Demarest of New York, and is lined with rose-colored corduroy. (Photo by June Fallaw)

Everyone is familiar with the song about the surrey with the fringe on top. A country vehicle and a very comfortable one, this was used for picnics, going to church, and any other similar occassion. (Photo by June Fallaw)

This is one form of "doctor's buggy." Other types had more hoodlike tops. In both types the tops could be folded back in good weather and these were the predecessors of today's "convertibles." (Photo by June Fallaw)

The hansom cab was the original taxi. Above the passenger's head is a little trap door which can be pushed up and through which the driver and passenger can communicate. (Photo by June Fallaw)

Another type of commercial vehicle
was the package wagon. This type,
with a pair, was also used by depart-
ment stores to make deliveries in the
city. Note the beautifully matched
chestnuts. Wanamaker's in the old
days identified their delivery wagons
not only by discreetly placed lettering
as shown here, but also by their horses
which were always matched dapple
grays. (Photo by June Fallaw)

Outside the arena the six-horse hitch of matched Clydesdales are readied for their exhibition. These horses are owned and shown by Louis Silva of Circle S Empire Ranch of Hayward, California.

The horses enter at a spanking trot, all in step. Not only are they matched in body color, but all have white stockings to the knees which help to display the heavy "feathers" which cover the lower legs and fetlock joints.

After circling the ring, the team is halted, then backed up in such a manner that the wagon is against the wall and at right angles to the track.

Without moving forward, the team two-tracks to the left . . .

. . . the leaders cutting in towards the wall . . .

. . . until the whole team is straightened out at right angles to the wagon, parallel to the "curb."

They then step back to the right, the
back wheels remaining stationary . . .

. . . the horses continuing to move
to the right until they are at right
angles to the body of the wagon with
the front wheels cut completely under.
This type of maneuver was essential
when all deliveries were made by
team, and a wagon had to be backed
up to the curb for unloading, and
horses moved out of the center of the
street so that other vehicles might pass.

The team now trots down to the opposite end of the arena where two posts have been placed. These posts are somewhat nearer together than the combined length of team and horses. The driver must now drive a figure eight around the posts without breaking the trot of the wheel horses. (The leaders must often canter on the turns.)

A sharp cut to the left with the rim of the back wheel almost touching the post starts the figure.

Then a sudden cut back to the right, the leaders cantering around the second post.

Now the team is straightened out to go back around the first post.

Mission accomplished, the team trots
out of the arena.

Fire Engine

One of the most delightful exhibitions put on at the Santa Barbara
Show was the one showing how old-time fire departments handled an
emergency. We first got a view of the fire engine being polished up for
its performance in Chapter One. Now let's see it in action.

Its polished brass glittering and live
steam billowing from its boiler, the
fire engine circles the arena. This
engine was built in 1878 and was
found in Lewiston, Maine, a few years
ago where it was still being used by
the Peck Store to thaw frozen pipes.
It is an Amoskeag, size number two,
and, as far as could be ascertained,
the only one of its kind still operable.
After being bought by the Poppy Hill
Pottery firm, it was completely
renovated.

183

As the fire engine draws up to the hydrant the hand-drawn hose cart pulls in behind it.

In the final act of the performance, the stalwart firemen led by their bugler direct a spray of water at the realistically burning building while a photographer somewhat handicapped by the smokey haze, takes a picture.